YOU CHOOSE BOOKS

The
QUEEN
MARY

A CHILLING INTERACTIVE ADVENTURE

by Matt Doeden

CAPSTONE PRESS
a capstone imprint

You Choose Books are published by Capstone Press,
1710 Roe Crest Drive, North Mankato, Minnesota 56003
www.mycapstone.com

Library of Congress Cataloging-in-Publication Data
Names: Doeden, Matt, author.
Title: The Queen Mary : a chilling interactive adventure / by Matt Doeden
Description: North Mankato, Minnesota : Capstone Press, [2017] | Series:
You choose books. you choose: haunted places | Includes bibliographical
  references and index.
Identifiers: LCCN 2016007073| ISBN 9781515725787 (library binding) | ISBN
  9781515725824 (ebook pdf)
Subjects: LCSH: Queen Mary (Steamship)–Juvenile literature.
  Ghosts–Juvenile literature. | Plot-your-own stories.
Classification: LCC BF1486 .D64 2017 | DDC 133.1/22–dc23
LC record available at http://lccn.loc.gov/2016007073

Editorial Credits
Mari Bolte, editor; Heidi Thompson, designer; Wanda Winch, media researcher;
Laura Manthe, production specialist

Photo Credits
Alamy: Matthew Richardson, 11, 32; Courtesy of The Queen Mary, 18, 38, 43, 48, 53, 70,
102, 104; David Zanzinger Unique Stock Photography, 28, 34, 40, 75, 80; Dreamstime:
Imdan, 8, 16, Jruffa, 98, Wangkun Jia, 66, 86; Library of Congress: Prints and Photographs
Division, 60; Lisa Sikorski, 94; Long Island Paranormal Investigators, 62, 77; Mike Darling,
50; Shutterstock: happykanppy, old paper painting design, Jhaz Photography, 56, Nejron
Photo, cover (top), 1, Plateresca, grunge label design, run4it, grunge ink painting design,
saki80, grunge frame design, Tom Tom, 82, trekandshoot, 14; SuperStock: Pantheon/
Mar/Illustrated London News, Ltd, 97; Thinkstock: Getty Images/David McNew, cover
(bottom), 4, 24, Paul Erickson, 6; U.S. Navy photo, 100; Wikimedia: David Krieger, 90

Printed in Canada.
009633F16

Table of Contents

INTRODUCTION

YOU are alone aboard the historic *Queen Mary*, a grand ship with a rich history ... a *deadly* history. As storm winds howl outside, you're about to find out why this ship is known as one of the most haunted places in the world. Your choices will guide the story. Will you run? Will you hide? Or will you stand up to unlock the haunted mysteries of the *Queen Mary*? Turn the page to find out.

The *Queen Mary* served during World War II (1939–1945). She was the largest and fastest troopship during that time.

WELCOME ABOARD

You can't help but laugh. "This place is supposed to be haunted?" you ask your older brother Cody. You stand on the deck of the famous ship, the *Queen Mary*, following along behind a tour guide. The guide is explaining that the ship once carried enemy prisoners of war. It's interesting, but you find yourself tuning her out. Your parents have always been history buffs, and you've been all over the world, touring this historical site or that one. At some point, all of the tours start to sound the same to you.

At first, when your parents told you that you'd be visiting the *Queen Mary* during your trip to California, you were excited. *A haunted ship!* Who wouldn't be interested in that? You imagined dark, creepy corridors, creaking hinges, and cold, clammy gusts wafting over the deck.

Turn the page.

But in reality, the lifeboats are lined up in a neat row, gleaming under the bright sunshine. The ship's bridge sparkles. The floors are spotless, the air warm and humid, and there are tourists everywhere. It's not even a proper ship anymore—instead, it's a hotel. The "scary ship" has become the ultimate tourist trap. What a letdown. The basement in your own house seems more haunted than this place.

The total recreation area on the *Queen Mary* is comparable in size to a football stadium.

"You're all very lucky," the tour guide is saying. "Today is the last day the ship is open, at least for a while. Starting tomorrow, she's undergoing major renovations and repairs. Things will be closed for about a month."

"Let's get out of here," Cody tells you during a break. You eagerly agree. You find your parents, who are deep in a debate about which ship was grander—the *Queen Mary* or the RMS *Titanic*.

"Mom, Dad," Cody interrupts. "We're thinking about bailing. Can we hit the beach and meet you back at the hotel tonight?"

Your dad looks annoyed, but your mom quickly agrees. That's the nice thing about having an 18-year-old brother. Your parents are usually willing to let the two of you do your own thing.

Turn the page.

The two of you head off, leaving your parents to their ship debate. "Can we rent a surfboard?" you ask.

Cody makes a face. "I was really thinking I'd rather just watch people."

You groan, knowing what that means. "People watching" means that Cody wants to go looking for girls. You can think of about one thing worse than finishing this tour—watching your awkward brother try to talk to girls.

"Fine," you tell Cody. "Go do your thing. Good luck meeting someone interesting." Cody flashes a big grin, claps you playfully on the shoulder, and is gone in a flash.

You may be staying, but that doesn't mean you plan to go back to the tour. You've got at least 30 minutes of freedom. Time to explore.

You mill around the Promenade Deck, then take an elevator down to a lower deck. You press a button at random, and the elevator takes you to a floor deep inside the ship. "Now this is more like it," you say, stepping out of the elevator into a small, dark corridor. A sign pointing to the Boiler Room catches your attention. You start down that way.

The ship's interior design, including the elevators, draws heavily from the Art Deco style that was popular around the time the ship was built.

Turn the page.

It appears that some of the renovations have already begun down here. Paint has been stripped from the walls. Electrical wires hang bare from the ceiling.

You're busy staring up at a nasty knot of wiring when you trip over an empty bucket. You fall hard, cracking your head on the floor.

For a moment, you lie there, stunned. Stars dance before your eyes. Your whole world is spinning. You try to stand but feel suddenly lightheaded and dizzy. You lower yourself back onto the floor. You'll just close your eyes for a moment to get yourself together ...

You wake later, in the dark. Your head is pounding and your muscles ache. You groan, roll over, and look at your watch. It's 10:30. At night! Your heart races. You've been down here for hours!

Despite the headache, you seem otherwise unhurt. With a groan, you pull yourself up. You make your way back to the elevator and return to the Promenade Deck. As you step outside, thunder rumbles and a strong wind howls through the night. Lightning flashes light the sky. There's not a soul in sight. You grab your cell phone, but a notification window blinks, "NO SERVICE."

That's when you hear the screaming.

To investigate, turn to page 14.

To get off the ship as soon as possible, turn to page 16.

You shudder. The sound is a long, drawn-out wail. It sounds like a person in terrible pain.

It's just the howling wind, you think. But you don't really believe it. The sound is coming from the bow of the ship. Overhead, a bright flash of lightning is followed almost immediately by a crash of thunder. You feel the ship shudder under your feet. At that moment, every light—inside and out—flickers, and then goes out.

The *Queen Mary* measures 1,020 feet (311 meters) long.

You freeze. Another lightning bolt streaks through the sky. The air feels electric. You hear a rush in the distance, out over the sea. The storm is about to hit, and it's going to pack a punch. You're still curious what's making that terrible noise up ahead, but you realize that being outside might be a major mistake.

To duck inside, turn to page 18.

To brave the elements and continue forward to the bow, turn to page 56.

You shudder at the sound. The scream sounds human—but it also sounds different somehow. The sound chills you to your very core. The hairs on your arms stand straight up, as if charged by electricity.

Let's see. A haunted ship. A nasty bump on the head. And now this otherworldly screaming.

Even permanently docked, the *Queen Mary* still floats on the water. It rises and falls several feet every day with the tide.

That's all you need to know. You're in no mood for adventure. Better to get back to your hotel room and crack open a nice, safe book.

There's one major problem. The ship's gangways have been lifted. There's no easy way to get off. Only a small strip of water separates the ship from the dock, but the water is far below. It's cold, black, and churning from the storm winds.

To head to the lobby to look for a phone, turn to page 23.

To dive in and swim for it, turn to page 68.

Your curiosity will have to wait. This storm is going to be bad. You throw open the first door you find and duck inside.

The door slams shut behind you, and the darkness is almost crushing. Your heart races and you attempt to step back outside before you gather your wits and remember—you've got your phone! It may not be able to get a signal, but it can serve as a flashlight. You breathe a sigh of relief as its dim glow lights the passage.

As many as 150 different spirits have been reported aboard the *Queen Mary*, making it one of the most haunted places in the world.

Well, you tell yourself, *I did want an adventure on a haunted ship.*

You creep along slowly, swinging your phone back and forth. It casts an eerie light, with long, dancing shadows all around you. You can hear the storm raging on outside. The ship is well secured, but even so, the deck beneath your feet feels unsteady.

You pass a stairwell. A hanging sign on the door lists the decks you can access. The first one to catch your attention is the engine room. *Now that might be interesting,* you think. Then you notice B Deck. This deck is three levels below the Promenade Deck and contains many of the ship's staterooms. Something about that jogs your memory.

Turn the page.

You think back to your tour earlier today. Before you left, the guide had said something about B Deck ... about one of the cabins. B340. That was it. The guide said it was the most haunted place on the ship. The hotel operators aboard the ship won't even rent the room out anymore. If it's ghosts you're after, that might be the place to start.

To head to the engine room, go to page 21.

To seek out the famous room B340, turn to page 28.

With a quick check of your phone's battery—still more than half charged—you take a deep breath and start to head down into the dark lower decks. The deeper you descend into the ship, the creepier things feel. Every crack and creak seems louder and more ominous.

As you step out into the wider hallway, your phone's light reveals a place that looks nothing like the ornate upper decks. Instead of warm, polished wood, you're greeted with cold, gritty metal. The deck is crisscrossed with a maze of pipes and beams. Every step sends a sharp echo through the corridor.

Just then, your phone enters sleep mode. As you reach to flip it back on, you freeze. The power is out and your phone's screen is black. That means it should be pitch dark. Yet, you can still see. You squint. There's no denying it.

Turn the page.

There's a light up ahead. It's a cool, blue light, and it seems to be wavering and flickering, reminding you of the light from a candle.

You shiver. Suddenly, you feel very cold. Faint laughter begins to echo down the metal hallway.

To turn around and get out of there as fast as you can, turn to page 26.

To continue toward the engine room to investigate, turn to page 42.

The light of your phone barely cuts through the darkness in the lobby. During the day, the lobby seemed warm and spacious. Now in blackness it feels small and claustrophobic. Frantically, you shine your phone, its pale cone of light leading you to the lobby's front desk.

There! A phone sits just behind the desk. You grab the receiver. But there's no dial tone. Frustrated, you drop your head into your hands. As you sit there trying to work out what to do next, a faint whisper tickles your ear.

You can't make out any words. You can't even figure out which direction it's coming from. But it's unmistakably a whisper. It sends a chill up your spine. *I have to get off this ship*, you tell yourself. *I think I'm going mad.*

Turn the page.

You notice something on the far wall. It's a large photo of the docked ship. You shine your light on it for a better view.

The *Queen Mary* measures 181 feet (55.2 meters) from the top of the first funnel to the bottom of the boat's keel.

A line of gangways connect the ship to the dock. But you already know that the ramps have been removed for the restoration. What catches your eye is the steel cable that runs from the prow of the ship down to solid ground. The cable helps anchor the ship in place. You might be able to use that line to get off the ship. It's a crazy idea. But is it any crazier than staying on a haunted ship alone all night?

To head for the anchoring lines, turn to page 86.

To try to find a safe place to hide for the night, turn to page 90.

"No thanks," you mutter, backing away. A spooky adventure is one thing. Walking into a weird blue light at the heart of a historically haunted ship is quite another. You may be a thrill-seeker, but you're not stupid. You've seen horror movies before.

You don't waste any time climbing back up to the higher decks. The farther you get from the engine room and that strange light, the better you feel. You take some deep breaths in relief. Part of you feels relieved to be away from it. But another part feels just a little regretful. What might you have seen there? You'll never know now.

As you walk up the stairwell, you notice a sign marked "B Deck." It's not too late to go check out B340. You hesitate. If the engine room spooked you, how are you going to handle a place that's supposed to be even more haunted?

Maybe it would be better if you just headed up to the Promenade Deck where you'll be safer.

To seek out B340, turn to page 28.

To head up to the Promenade Deck to wait for morning, turn to page 80.

Curiosity wins. The most haunted room on the ship? You've got to see that.

As soon as you step out into the corridor, you begin to feel uneasy. You've never been claustrophobic. But by the cool, dim light of your phone, the tight spaces inside the *Queen Mary* suddenly have you feeling trapped. You shake your head and tell yourself it's just your imagination running wild.

Even the hallways of the *Queen Mary* are rumored to be haunted.

You creep down the corridor, following the signs to B340. You're not quite sure what you expected, but when you arrive, you can't help but feel a bit disappointed. The door to the supposedly haunted stateroom looks just like any other. You put your hand on the doorknob and give it a test. To your shock, it's not locked. You take a deep breath. Your hands are shaking, but you want to see inside.

Something crashes down the corridor. You pull your hand back instinctively and spin toward the noise. At first, you can't see anything. But you can feel something there in the darkness. Something light. A shape.

You can't breathe. Your heart races. The pale figure moves closer and closer. It begins to take the shape of a person. It's a child—a little girl.

Turn the page.

The girl seems to flicker, appearing solid and then fading to almost nothing a moment later. She stares at you, then turns toward the door. Slowly, she looks back at you and shakes her head, mouthing the word, "No."

Then she's gone. Just like that, you're all alone in the corridor again. A sudden wave of sadness weighs you down.

To continue down the corridor to look for the ghost, go to page 31.

To enter B340, turn to page 59.

Your hands are trembling. Your breathing is shallow and rapid. *What was that?*

The stories are true. The *Queen Mary* is haunted, and one of the ghosts has just communicated with you. The little girl's message was crystal clear. Without a second glance, you leave B340 behind. You shudder when you wonder what sort of spirit you might have encountered in there.

You continue down the corridor, in the direction that the ghost appeared. You don't see anything, but every few minutes, you swear you hear giggling. Is it real? Or is your imagination really running away from you now?

You follow the sounds until you reach an area marked POOL.

Turn the page.

Visitors have reported hearing knocking and clanging around the first-class swimming pool doors.

As you step inside, the entire ship seems to heave under your feet, as if it was suddenly set adrift again.

Impossible! The ship has been docked since the late 1960s! Yet the feeling of motion is unmistakable.

Your vision blurs. Everything seems hazy, as if a fog just rolled in. You shake your head and rub your eyes. When you open them again, you're shocked by what you see. The fog is still there, but the room has changed. It looks as it must have half a century ago. You hear the sound of a child laughing and splashing in the water. You sense, but can't see, others in the area as well. It's as if you're only being allowed to see what someone—some*thing*—wants you to see. You're dimly aware that you can no longer hear the rumble of thunder outside.

As you look around, you realize that the laughter has stopped. You move toward the pool. It feels more like floating than walking. You can't see anything. There's splashing and then a desperate gasp. You hear a panicked voice, screaming, "Jackie! Jackie!"

Turn the page.

Then, in an instant, all is still. The scene around you fades. The distant rumble of thunder returns. The scene seems to crumble around you, and the room is empty.

Almost empty.

Female ghosts are said to haunt the first-class swimming pool.

On the far side of the pool stands a figure. The ghost, who you now realize is Jackie, clings to a tattered doll. She looks straight at you and speaks. Her words are like wind, but there is no mistaking them. "I want my mommy."

To answer Jackie, turn to page 36.

To run toward her, turn to page 40.

The shape across the room looks at you. Her definition seems to flicker, fading at times, then growing stronger. Yet as you stare at this figure, it almost doesn't seem like a ghost. It seems like a little girl, alone and afraid. You feel a swell of emotions—sadness, loss, loneliness. It's overwhelming.

"I want to help you, Jackie!" you call, your voice cracking. The words echo off the walls, making the room seem very empty.

Jackie is fading. But before the figure disappears completely, you're certain you see her smile. For several long moments, you find yourself just staring at the place where she stood. She seemed so small and alone. You try to talk yourself into the idea that this is all in your head. But you know better.

You're going to be stuck on this ship for the night, you realize. You glance at your phone—not quite midnight. Plenty of time to help Jackie. When you came to this ship, you wanted a close encounter with ghosts. Well, you got one. If you're locked on a haunted ship all night, you're going to make the most of it. You'll be the one to find Jackie's mother.

Shaken but thrilled, you make your way back to the lobby to start searching for answers. The storm rages on outside, though the worst of it seems to have passed. As you move slowly through the ship's dark corridors, you keep your ears open. At one point, you're certain you hear footsteps behind you. You whirl around, but can't see anything. You swear you hear someone giggling in the distance.

Turn the page.

As you step into the Grand Lobby, which is dimly lit by emergency lighting, you feel like you're stepping back in time. From its intricate woodwork to the ornate front desk, the lobby really makes you feel like you're a traveler from the first half of the 20th century. Down the hallway from the lobby, you find a bookshelf. There, you hit the jackpot—a book all about the ship and its ghosts.

One ghost story states that the ship's purser—the employee responsible for the money onboard—was murdered. He worked in the lobby, but his ghost haunts room B340.

By the light of your phone, you start to read. Soon, you're lost in the pages, learning about the ship's history as a passenger liner, its service during World War II, and the tragedies that befell many of its passengers. Several passages capture your attention. One tells of the ghost of a young woman reported in a lounge called the Queen's Salon. Another tells of the Lady in White, a woman seen throughout the ship—often in the lobby itself. You wonder if the women are related in some way. Finally, there's the third-class playroom, where visitors have reported hearing the cries of an infant.

To search for the Lady in White, turn to page 45.

To investigate the Queen's Salon, turn to page 49.

To seek out the playroom, turn to page 52.

Your heart is racing. You have to act. Without hesitating, you dash across the tiled floor, rushing toward the figure of the child. But by the time you get there, she's gone. There's nobody here. You look down in frustration. That's when you spot the footprints.

You kneel down, touching your fingers to the floor. The footprints are wet. Yet the pool, which hasn't been used in years, is bone dry.

Stories say Jackie died in the second-class pool, which was removed when the ship went out of service in 1968. The first-class pool is still open for guests to tour.

Am I losing my mind?

In the distance, you hear a giggle. A cool breeze wafts across the room. You shiver. The footprints lead away from the pool. You follow them to where they stop, right in front of the womens' dressing room door.

The pool room is dark, yet there seems to be a faint blue light seeping out from beneath the door. You put your hand on the door. It's cold, and it seems to vibrate very slightly. Something about this place feels very, very wrong. Yet, this is where the footsteps lead. If you want to follow, this is the way to go.

To enter the room, turn to page 62.

To leave the pool and return to the Promenade Deck, turn to page 65.

Laughter? Strange blue light? What is this? You know you'll never forgive yourself if you don't find out. So with a gulp, you walk slowly forward. You do your best to step lightly, but every footstep seems to echo through the corridor like the rumbles of distant thunder outside.

The laughter grows louder, and the cold blue light gets brighter. As you round a corner, you freeze in your tracks, your breath caught in your chest. You can't believe your eyes. It's not possible. You shake your head and rub your eyes, but the figures are still there. Two sailors, clear as day. Yet you know they can't be real, because you can see right through them.

You wanted ghosts. You've found them.

You stand before a passage marked Watertight Door 13. The two figures are jumping back and forth through the door as it slowly closes shut. One of them turns and stares directly at you.

The watertight doors were sealed during emergencies. Sailors would make a game of jumping in and out of the doorways as the doors closed.

Turn the page.

It's a young man with sharp features and a whisper of a beard. But his eyes are what seizes your attention. They're like deep, black pits. Blacker than black. You feel like you're staring into nothing. The ghost smiles and motions with a finger. He wants you to join in the game!

The hatch is half closed. You realize that they're playing a game of chicken. The ghostly sailors are seeing who can be the last to slip through the heavy metal hatch. Their laughter, once lighthearted, now sounds more like wailing.

A game of chicken with two ghosts? You must be going crazy. But when in your life will you ever get such a chance again?

To join the game, turn to page 76.

To hold your ground, turn to page 78.

"The Lady in White," you whisper. Something about her seems mystical and exciting. Could she be Jackie's mother? You want to find out.

According to the book, the Lady in White roams the ship's corridors at night. She often appears in or near the lobby. So you'll do the same. At first, you walk slowly through the halls by the light of your phone. Every time you round a corner, you expect to see her. But nothing.

You flick off the phone and sit down, leaning against one of the corridor walls. Perhaps the Lady in White will come to you. You wait … and wait … and wait.

"This isn't happening," you mutter, stretching tired muscles as you stand up. As you reach to turn on your phone and leave, you catch movement out of the corner of your eye.

Turn the page.

You whirl, staring down the corridor. *There!* Up ahead! You see her!

A chill traces your spine, and you cannot suppress a shudder. The ghost seems to be moving slowly in your direction. She is so clear … so real. Despite everything you've seen, you almost can't believe what you're looking at. And you know nobody else ever will—that is, at least not without proof.

That's when you realize you've still got your phone in hand. With a few taps, you could have all the proof you'll ever need.

To quietly watch and follow the Lady in White, go to page 47.

To snap a picture and get evidence of what you've seen, turn to page 94.

You're not here to take pictures. You wanted to find the Lady in White, and you've found her.

The ghost seems not to notice you as she moves through the corridors. She floats above the ground. The glow that surrounds her sometimes fades and flickers, but never quite goes out.

It's a slow crawl through the dark corridors. You keep back but never let the apparition out of your sight. As you round a corner, a sharp, shrill sound grows in intensity—a baby's cry! You realize that the Lady is moving toward the third-class playroom. Is she leading you here? Is this some sort of message?

The figure stops. She turns toward the playroom. It's unmistakable—the crying is coming from beyond this door. The Lady in White turns again and looks at you.

Turn the page.

For the first time, she seems to acknowledge your presence. Then slowly, she disappears. Her message is clear. She wants you to go into the playroom.

Turn to page 53.

Some guests claim to have heard a baby's cry from inside the third-class playroom.

The Queen's Salon must have once been a sight to behold. It's a huge space with several fireplaces, polished marble floors, and a central stage covered by long golden drapes. As you cast the light of your phone around the room, you can't help but imagine what it must have been like more than half a century ago. You find yourself imagining well-dressed, first-class passengers mingling about, eating and drinking as a band plays a gentle tune.

The image in your head is so clear that you can almost see it. With a chill, you realize that you *can* see it! With a swipe, you turn off your phone. Yet a pale yellow light hangs over the Queen's Salon. The scene becomes more real when the sound of gentle whispers reaches your ears. It's just at the limit of your hearing, so faint you're not even sure they're really there.

Turn the page.

Both the Queen's Salon and the Royal Salon are decorated with large tapestries.

A cool breeze wafts through the room, giving you goosebumps. You turn and see that an ornate wood dance floor has appeared. Your breath catches in your chest. There, a figure dressed in white floats above the dance floor.

The dancer gently spins, wheels, and dips. All alone, and to a tune no one else can hear. Something about her makes you feel intensely sad. You step toward the dance floor.

You watch her, mesmerized. Time seems to freeze. You find her movements hypnotic.

After a minute or an hour, she stops. She turns to stare straight at you. She extends a wispy, white hand. You can't quite make out her face, but it seems that she might be smiling at you. It's an invitation.

To dance with her, turn to page 70.

To turn and run, turn to page 74.

As you make your way through the ship, shining the light of your phone in every direction, you can't help but shudder. You start to imagine ghostly shapes in every light flicker. At one point, you're sure you hear footsteps behind you. Another time, it's a low moaning, as if someone is in terrible pain. You tell yourself it's just the ship creaking, but that doesn't make the tingle in your spine go away.

One sound is unmistakable. It's a baby's cry. It's a cold, eerie sound, almost like a recording of a recording. And it's coming from the third-class playroom. You hesitate for a moment outside the door. *It's now or never*, you tell yourself.

Go to page 53.

You step into the playroom, half expecting to find a crib with the wailing ghost of an infant. But the moment you cross the doorway, the crying stops. One of the walls is covered in a huge mural, once colorful but now faded and dull. An old blackboard stands against one wall.

The ship had playrooms for first-, second-, and third-class travelers. The first-class playroom had holes for hiding, washable walls, and a slide.

Turn the page.

You take it all in for a few moments, waiting for the sound of the baby crying to start again. You strain, hoping to hear something, anything. But the room remains silent.

As you turn to leave, you feel a sudden chill. Goosebumps cover your arms. Your breath fogs up in front of your face.

The white figure seems to materialize out of nothing. At first, it looks like little more than a human-shaped cloud. But the cloud forms and becomes more detailed, soon resembling a young mother cradling a child. The child appears limp in her arms. *Just sleeping,* you tell yourself. But something about the figure makes you feel intensely sad. The woman's face appears distraught. Her eyes are deep, hollow sockets.

She opens her mouth. The wail that comes out sounds like it comes from another world. Your skin crawls. Your knees start to buckle. Her sadness and rage is so deep it feels like a living thing.

The ghost begins to move. Then it turns toward you.

To run, turn to page 74.

To try to communicate with the spirit, turn to page 82.

You glance to the east. Arcs of lightning light up the sky, revealing huge thunderheads. They're bearing down on you fast. You have to hurry. Navigating by the near constant pulses of lightning, you rush forward.

The blast of wind at the front of the storm hits just as you reach the bow, nearly knocking you down. Sheets of rain, blowing nearly sideways, follow. You lift your arm to cover your face as best you can.

Warm Pacific waters can generate powerful thunderstorms.

Despite the howl of the wind and the crashing of thunder, the screaming is louder than ever. You rush to the railing. You know it's foolish to be out here, but you have to know.

You lean over the rail. At first, you see nothing in the blackness. For a moment, the screaming stops as your eyes scan the dark waves.

Just as you're about to give up and turn around, something catches your attention. It's a dark shape. It looks like it's just above the water's surface.

Waves crash against the ship's hull. You lean over more and more, trying to make sense of what you see.

It all happens in an instant. An especially bright flash of lightning reveals the shape surging up and taking a human form in front of you.

Turn the page.

It's a sailor, thin, broken, and utterly pale. It opens its mouth and screams. You feel something like cold, clammy fingers wrap around your wrist. Then you feel a pull. A gust of wind blasts over the ship, and suddenly you're falling …

The next day, a police investigator finds your body washed ashore. "Must have been blown overboard by the wind," she says with a sigh. She doesn't notice the strange, finger-shaped bruises on your arms as she covers you with her jacket.

THE END

To follow another path, turn to page 13.
To learn more about the Queen Mary, *turn to page 99.*

You stand there for a moment outside B340. Your mind races. Did you really just see that? Or is your mind playing tricks on you? You did take a pretty good bump on the head earlier. And this place could just be letting your imagination run wild. Yet, it felt so real.

Your legs begin to buckle at the thought. You need to sit down. You swallow hard, then turn the knob and throw open the door. You half expect something horrible to happen. To your relief and disappointment, nothing happens. It's just a room, walls pristine white, bed neatly made.

Suddenly confused, you plop down on the bed, holding your head in your hands. You try to catch your breath and calm your nerves. Everything seems to be spinning.

Turn the page.

Over your shoulder, you feel a presence.
A draft? Indoors? But it's definitely there.
You're sure of it.

Then you hear a whisper. You can't make out
the words. But you know you heard something.

Something brushes your back.

Around 4,000 men worked on the *Queen Mary*. She launched
on September 26, 1934. More than 15,000 people paid to see
the ship beforehand.

You scream and bolt from the bed. There's something wrong here—something foul in the air. But before you can leave, icy fingers grasp your arm. An invisible hand drags you down and no matter how hard you pull, you can't get free. As you're pulled to the floor, visions flash through your mind. This room … someone trapped … terrible anger …

As you struggle, a figure emerges over you. The scarred face of the man is terrifying. His hair hangs over his face and his mouth is twisted open. You try to scream, but it feels like a hand is squeezing the air from your lungs. The ghost's face is inches from your own. Its cold breath reeks of rotten meat and death. It smiles, and whispers the last sound you ever hear: *Mine.*

THE END

To follow another path, turn to page 13.
To learn more about the Queen Mary, turn to page 99.

Your hands seem to freeze as you start to push the door open. It's as if your body is fighting you, as if some instinct deep in your bones is telling you to run. You imagine you hear a high-pitched scream inside your head.

You pause, take a deep breath, and collect yourself. With resolve, you push the door open and step inside.

The doors to the womens' changing room for the first-class swimming pool are rumored to be a gateway to another dimension.

The air is like ice. Within seconds, you're shivering, clutching your arms to your body. Shaking, you look around. No sign of footprints.

"Jackie?" you whisper. "Jackie?" A little louder. Finally, you shout it, your voice cracking in the cold. "Jackie! Are you here?"

Just feet in front of you, a ball of blue light appears. Tiny sparks, like lightning, wriggle and writhe around it. The ball crackles and hisses. Then it begins to grow.

You scream and turn to run. But at that moment, icy fingers grasp your ankle. You stumble, crashing onto the floor. Your head makes a cracking sound as it hits the hard tile beneath.

Turn the page.

Your vision blurs. Your senses dull. But they're not dull enough. You're painfully aware of every moment as that terrible ball of blue light and raw energy envelops you. Your breathing slows, and then stops, as the light suffocates you. You feel every second as it seems to rip you from this world. Things go black as the light carries you somewhere dark and cold and very lonely. Your consciousness fades. You're slipping … slipping … fading out. Gone.

THE END

To follow another path, turn to page 13.
To learn more about the Queen Mary, *turn to page 99.*

You step back from the door. Every sense is telling you to get away. After all you've seen tonight, you're not about to ignore that. With one final glance around the empty pool room, you turn and leave as quickly as you can.

Back in the dark corridors, you realize that you've been holding your breath. You let it out slowly. You fall to one knee, shaking, suddenly terrified. You need to get out of here, now.

You half walk, half run to the nearest stairwell and return to the Promenade Deck. Outside, a steady rain still falls, but the worst of the storm's violence has passed. You slide onto the floor and rest your head on your knees. Without intending to, you nod off and fall asleep.

Workers find you there the next morning. Within minutes, you're loaded into an ambulance and rushed to a hospital.

Turn the page.

One lap around the Promenade Deck is equal
to a quarter mile (0.4 kilometers).

When your terrified parents arrive, you let
it all spill out—the strange sounds, the figures.
Jackie, that terrible blue light. Everything.

"You had quite a bump on the head," says
your doctor as she shines a light into your eyes.
"It looks like you have a concussion. What you
saw was probably just hallucinations caused by a
bruise to your brain. It's not at all uncommon."

"It was real," you insist. But everyone just smiles and nods without listening. Then they tell you to rest. They don't believe you. And as the days pass and your headaches fade, you begin to second-guess yourself.

But one thing is for sure. When you close your eyes every night, all you can see is the face of a lonely and frightened little girl who misses her mother.

THE END

To follow another path, turn to page 13.
To learn more about the Queen Mary, *turn to page 99.*

The water may be cold and a storm may be coming. But you're not staying on this ship one second longer. You shove your phone in your pocket, look down at the black water below, and take a deep breath.

You count to three, and then you dive. It's a long way down. You have just enough time to question whether this was a good idea.

You hit the water with surprising force. As your head slams against the ocean surface, it feels like you've run into a wall. You were already a little lightheaded from the nasty knock you took to the head before. Now, as you find yourself immersed in the black ocean water, you are completely disoriented. You can't tell which way is up. You force your eyes open—just in time to see a ghostlike face in front of yours. The figure beckons to you, and you follow it.

Too late, you realize it's leading you down, not up. Panicked, you pump your arms and legs to return to the surface. But your clothes weigh you down, and you try to kick them off. Shadows wrap themselves around your wrists and ankles, pulling you deeper. You struggle, and your lungs begin to ache. You open your mouth to scream. Water rushes in through your nose and mouth as you are pulled into the ocean's depths. You cannot escape.

THE END

To follow another path, turn to page 13.
To learn more about the Queen Mary, *turn to page 99.*

You stare at the ghostly figure before you. She waits patiently, hand extended. You take a deep breath and step onto the wooden dance floor.

From the first moment, she seems less like a ghost and more like a flesh-and-blood person. Her hand is warm in yours. And now, suddenly, her face is bright. Her eyes are a stunning emerald. The room around you seems alive, vibrant in a way it wasn't before.

Dining and dancing were historically a popular affair aboard the ship. Some of the dancers may have stayed onboard.

You don't know much about ballroom dancing, but the moves come naturally as you float around the dance floor. That's when you realize you can hear music—a slow, mournful melody. Together, you and the ghost spin and twirl. You find yourself getting lost in the dance.

With a bit of panic, you struggle to regain your grip on reality. You stop and take a step back. The music instantly fades. The young woman looks at you and nods.

"Jackie," you whisper, as if speaking too loudly will make all of this disappear. "A little girl in the pool. Do you know her? Are you her mother?"

The young woman closes her eyes, almost imperceptibly shakes her head. She lifts a single finger, placing it against your lips. The music begins again.

Turn the page.

You need to go. You can feel it, in the back of your mind. You want to move. You do. But for some reason, you can't bring yourself to step away. There's something comforting, so … right about staying. It's as if you're being swallowed up in the dance itself, entranced by its movements and its beauty. Part of you still wants to leave, but you push that desire aside. Because now you know you never will.

In the years that follow, guests of the *Queen Mary* marvel at her newest and most astonishing tale. The famous dancing woman in the Queen's Salon is no longer alone. Now, she appears with another dancer. Nobody knows where the mystery partner came from or who it might be. They can never quite make out the face.

Many people swear that when the dancers appear, they can hear the faint music and the sound of laughter. Visitors are warned not to linger too long, or risk getting caught in the dance too.

You are now and forever a part of the *Queen Mary's* collection.

THE END

To follow another path, turn to page 13.
To learn more about the Queen Mary, *turn to page 99.*

"What am I doing?" you mutter to yourself, staring at the apparition before you. This all seemed like an exciting adventure at first. But now it's something much worse. You've seen things that you know will haunt your dreams for the rest of your life. A sense of panic and suffocation falls over you. You suddenly want nothing more than to get out of here. Now.

You back away slowly at first, one slow step at a time. Gathering all of your courage, you turn and bolt in the other direction, too terrified to look back over your shoulder. It's a mad dash back to the Promenade Deck, and you're not sure which is louder, the thump of your footsteps or the pounding of your heart.

Bursting outside onto the Promenade Deck, you fall to your knees. Lightning flashes in the eastern sky, but the storm has passed.

You find a dry spot on the deck underneath a lifeboat, knowing there's no reasonable way off the ship. The hours stretch on, and it feels like dawn will never arrive. But of course, it does. And it doesn't take long before you're spotted by a shipyard employee.

Help is coming, and you can't wait to get off this haunted ship.

THE END

To follow another path, turn to page 13.
To learn more about the Queen Mary, *turn to page 99.*

Even the *Queen Mary's* sun deck is thought to be haunted.

A ghostly game of chicken? How can you resist? The ghost nods slowly at you as you approach. It points a single, bony finger toward the hatch. The other apparition doesn't even seem aware you're there. It continues to duck in and out of the closing hatch. There's only a few feet of opening left. You should be able to dart through and back again one time without any danger.

The steel flooring clangs as you approach. A low, grinding rumble of the closing door echoes off the bulkheads. You leap through. No problem! With a laugh you turn to jump back the other way. The hatch is closing faster than you thought. No time to waste.

You dart into the opening. But just as you leap, something grabs you. A cold, clammy hand wraps around your ankle. You fall forward, reaching toward the door's edge.

You're able to grip the opening for just a moment. Then you're pulled away. "No!" you scream, watching the watertight door close. "No!"

Everything goes dark. Even after the sound of your agonized screams fades away, the whisper of ghostly laughter echoes through the halls.

THE END

To follow another path, turn to page 13.
To learn more about the Queen Mary, *turn to page 99.*

The Watertight Door 13 ghost is said to haunt this area of the ship. He always disappears near the doorway.

Your feet feel like lead. There's no way you're jumping into a hatch on a haunted ship with two ghosts.

The figure beckons again. You shuffle backward, shaking your head. The hatch is slowly closing. The figure turns and dives through with inches to spare. You take a deep breath, believing that both ghosts will remain on the other side of the hatch. But at the last moment, one of them takes a leap. It's too late. The ghostly young sailor is trapped at the waist. You watch as the hatch crushes the terrified sailor. At the final moment, the sailor's agonized face looks toward you. He opens his mouth and screams.

An instant chill falls over the corridor. A blast of wind knocks you over. A dark shadow erupts from the dying sailor. It rises up, then violently sweeps over you in a wave of raw rage.

It's two days before workers find you, limp, shivering, and clinging to life. You're rushed to a hospital. Your body soon recovers. But your doctors can't explain what has happened to your mind. Your eyes stare blankly forward, never moving. Your face is contorted into an eternal scream. And no matter what they do, no matter how hard your parents try, nothing ever seems to bring you back. You may still be alive … technically. But the truth is that the *Queen Mary* has claimed yet another victim.

THE END

To follow another path, turn to page 13.
To learn more about the Queen Mary, *turn to page 99.*

With a shake of your head, you search for someplace safe to wait out the night. You thought you were up for a haunted adventure, but as it turns out, you'd really rather be safe at home. A scary book seems much safer. Heck, you're not even sure you're brave enough for *that* right now.

It's a lonely night. Every creak, bang, and bump makes you jump. You're on edge the whole time, but you don't see or hear anything that really points to ghosts.

The ghost of an officer is thought to haunt the ship's forward decks. Legend says he accidentally drank poison and he spends the afterlife searching for his murderer.

Maybe it was all just your imagination, you think as the night drags on. *Maybe I was scared for nothing.*

The workers find you the next morning. You're reunited with your family at the hospital, where you're treated for a concussion. You don't tell anyone what happened. "I must have gotten lost," you repeat over and over to those who ask.

Within a few weeks, your night alone aboard the famous *Queen Mary* is just a distant memory. You do think about it now and then. And sometimes you wish you'd decided to explore more, to learn a few of the ship's secrets. But there's no way you're ever going back.

THE END

To follow another path, turn to page 13.
To learn more about the Queen Mary, *turn to page 99.*

Every instinct in your body tells you to run.
But you came here for a reason—Jackie.

The ghost looms over you. Its mouth is
wide open, locked in its chilling cry. A feeling of
hopelessness and despair fills the room. It almost
cripples you. You have to act now, before it breaks
your will.

Strange figures, cold drafts, and whispers seem to linger in
every corner of the ship.

"I'm here for Jackie!" you shout over the spine-chilling noise.

In an instant, the ghost draws back, as if struck. The unearthly howl fades, and she seems to focus on you. *She understood that!*

"She's near the pool. I saw her. She ... she wants her mother. Can you help? Are you Jackie's mother?"

The ghost seems to grow smaller. The child in her arms fades away, as does the curtain of sorrow that had fallen over the room. Her features soften. She somehow looks younger.

She tilts her head, as if regarding you. She closes her eyes, then reaches out a hand to touch your shoulder. You feel an instant and intense chill at the touch. But while it's cold, it doesn't feel threatening. You believe it is a thank you.

Turn the page.

The figure fades from sight. You retreat into the corridor and fall to your knees, weeping. After a few moments, you pick yourself up, gather your emotions, and make your way to the pool area. As you approach, you hear the sound of laughter. It's Jackie. And she's not alone. There's another sound—a woman's laughter.

You throw open the doors to see. But when you step inside, the pool is empty. No ghosts, no visions. Just a strange feeling of peace and love. You find yourself soaking it in, just smiling. You'll head back up to the Promenade Deck to wait for morning. But first, you just want to bask in whatever's in the air.

You never forget your adventure on the *Queen Mary*. Years later, you return. "It's strange," says your tour guide. "For decades, the ghost of a young girl roamed this ship. Then suddenly, one day, she was gone. No one has seen or heard her since. I don't suppose we'll ever know why."

All you do is smile.

THE END

To follow another path, turn to page 13.
To learn more about the Queen Mary, *turn to page 99.*

You lean in closer, staring. The lines connect to the dock from the prow. They sweep down at a surprisingly sharp angle. But you're confident it's not too steep. *I can do this*, you tell yourself.

It's a mad dash to the prow. You half expect some ghostly hand to reach out and grab you at any moment. But aside from some ship-rattling cracks of thunder, nothing happens.

A Soviet Union submarine known as the *Scorpion* has been docked with the *Queen Mary* since 1998.

As you approach the bow, the screaming you heard earlier starts again. It's a human cry, but at the same time, it sounds almost animal. It's filled with pain and anger. The raw emotion of it hits you, momentarily locking all your muscles.

The rain pours down. Your clothes are soaked. Your hair is matted to your face. The near constant lightning makes it easy to find what you're looking for—the cable that leads off the ship. Now comes the hard part.

You strip out of your wet blue jeans. With a tug, you reassure yourself that they're strong enough. You take a deep breath, climb over the railing and drape the jeans over the steel cable. You wrap a pant leg around each wrist and grab onto the fabric as tightly as you can.

Turn the page.

The screaming grows louder. You make the mistake of looking down. Directly below you can see figures in the water. They look like dead bodies, but they are moving. Reaching. Wailing. Sharks or crocodiles would be a more welcome sight.

Don't let go! It's the only thought in your mind. The wet denim is hard to grip, but whatever you do, you can't let go.

You close your eyes, take a deep breath, block out the horrible screams, and leap forward. Hanging on for all you're worth, you slide down the cable like it's a zip line. Rain and wind batter your face, and your hands and arms ache from hanging on so tightly.

The descent feels endless, but you know it probably takes just a few seconds. *Only a little farther,* you think, ignoring your tired muscles.

Just when you think you can't hold on any longer, your feet connect with solid ground. Your momentum sends you spilling head over heels. The rough landing leaves you momentarily disoriented. It takes you a few moments to realize, *I made it!* The screams have faded away. All you can hear now is the pounding rain and the crashing thunder.

You climb back into your pants, which are shredded but better than nothing. It's time to go find your family. They're never going to believe this story.

THE END

To follow another path, turn to page 13.
To learn more about the Queen Mary, *turn to page 99.*

You shake your head. Have you lost it? Climbing down a steel cable? You're more likely to fall to your death than to actually escape. It's not worth the risk.

You head back inside and lock yourself in a stateroom. You grab a blanket off the bed and try to relax. But you jump at every bump, bang, and creak. Sometime after midnight, you drift off to sleep.

The ship's 346 original first-class staterooms are open to guests. No two rooms are alike.

When you wake up an hour later, you're groggy and confused. You're sure you heard a voice, though.

Someone stands in the doorway. Or, rather, some *thing*. It almost looks like a pale white shadow. As you stare, it becomes clearer and more defined. Eventually it takes the shape of a woman. You can see her features clearly. She's beautiful. And she's moving toward you.

You shuffle back, tripping over your own feet and sprawling to the floor. The ghost moves closer. You half-run, half-crawl in the other direction, cracking your head on an end table as you try to stand.

Turn the page.

Voices fill the ship. There are whispers, laughter, and screaming. You turn and run into the dark corridor, fumbling for your phone and its light. But in your panic, you drop it. You fall to the floor, desperately searching for it with your hands.

Something cold and damp connects with your hand. It feels like a dead fish. It smells even worse. You flinch.

The sound of slow, raspy breathing hisses across your ear. Then something touches your shoulder. It's a ghostly hand. Another grabs you. The voices grow louder. They are laughing.

You rise to your feet. Your legs feel like lead, but you charge away, bursting outside into the driving rain. The voices are following you. You can't hear anything else. Can't think of anything but running.

You rush to the railing. Without a moment's hesitation, you launch yourself over the edge and into darkness.

With the storm raging, no one notices the small figure plummeting toward the cold ocean water below. No one hears the splash. And no one comes to answer the garbled cries for help that follow.

THE END

To follow another path, turn to page 13.
To learn more about the Queen Mary, *turn to page 99.*

Slowly, you lift your phone. With a swipe, you bring up the camera and blast off three quick pictures.

In an instant, the Lady in White is gone. The corridor is empty. You rush toward the spot where you last saw her. You shiver—it's cold here. It feels like the temperature has dropped 20 degrees.

Today the *Queen Mary* offers several haunted tours featuring paranormal activity.

"No! Come back!" you shout. The words echo through the empty corridor. "I need your help! Please come back!"

She never does. With one mistake, your chance to help Jackie is gone.

You spend hours roaming the ship, searching and calling out for her, but you don't see anything paranormal for the rest of the night. She is gone. You make your way to the deck where you rest your head, heavy with guilt. Eventually you drift into a dreamless sleep.

Workers find you the next morning. Soon you're back with your family, and everything feels like a distant memory. Days pass before you think to check the photos on your phone.

Turn the page.

The first two show nothing but a dark blur. At first, the third one appears worthless as well. There's no ghost where the Lady in White was standing. But just before you hit delete, something in the far background captures your attention. *A face!* It's barely noticeable at first, but when you zoom in, it's unmistakable. It's a face. A child's face. *Jackie's face.*

"I'll come back, Jackie," you whisper. You don't know when or how, but you vow that someday, you'll keep your promise.

THE END

To follow another path, turn to page 13.
To learn more about the Queen Mary, *turn to page 99.*

On October 31, 1967, the *Queen Mary* set sail for the last time. She stopped in Spain, Brazil, Chile, Peru, Panama, and Mexico before coming to rest in Long Beach, California.

The modern-day *Queen Mary* is a floating hotel. Weddings, meetings, and other events take place there throughout the year.

EPILOGUE: THE *QUEEN MARY*

For hardcore ghost hunters, few places in the United States are more interesting than the *Queen Mary*. The grand British ship sailed the Atlantic Ocean for more than three decades, carrying everything from wealthy passengers to Allied soldiers to prisoners of war. Her history is laced with darkness and tragedy. Many believe the spirits of some who met their end aboard this grand ship linger there still.

The *Queen Mary* made her maiden voyage in 1936. At the time, she was among the grandest ships to sail the Atlantic. For three years, the ship carried passengers from actor Clark Gable to British Prime Minister Winston Churchill.

Then, in 1939, everything changed. World War II (1939–1945) broke out in Europe. The British and their allies needed all the ships they could get. That included the *Queen Mary*. She was called into service on March 1, 1940.

The ornate passenger ship was stripped to the bone to serve as a troop transporter. A new, colorless paint job earned the ship her wartime nickname—the *Grey Ghost*.

Nazi leader Adolf Hitler offered a $250,000 reward to anyone who could sink the *Queen Mary*.

The *Queen Mary* was a critical transport vessel for the British in a dark and bloody war. She also saw her fair share of tragedy. In one accident, the ship accidentally rammed a much smaller British vessel. The *Queen Mary* was under orders not to stop for any reason. The crew was forced to listen to the screams of the dying sailors they left behind.

The war ended in 1945 with an Allied victory. The *Queen Mary* was released from service and returned to her role as a luxury passenger ship. But the war left the world drastically changed. Technology was the new ruler of the world. Before the war, a ship was the only practical way to travel across the Atlantic Ocean. That was no longer true. Sleek airplanes were much faster, less costly, and were a new experience for many. The era of the luxury liner was ending.

The *Queen Mary* continued on for another 18 years, despite the dwindling demand for sea travel. Finally, in 1967, the *Queen Mary* was retired. For a time, it looked like the ship would be sold for scrap metal. But instead, a U.S. group bought the ship and brought it to Long Beach, California. The developers gutted much of the ship. The *Queen Mary* became a floating museum, and later, a hotel.

During the war, the *Queen Mary* carried more than 800,000 soldiers and sailed 600,000 miles (965,600 kilometers).

The *Queen Mary*'s travels were over. But her time as a tourist attraction was just beginning. The rumors of strange sightings began almost immediately. The mysterious Lady in White gave passengers the sense of the supernatural around every corner. Spooky chills and scary happenings in the famous cabin B340 included flying bedsheets, lights turning on and off on their own, and an angry ghost telling guests to get out. The reports became so common that the room is no longer rented out.

In the engine room, many reported seeing the spirit of a young man cut in half by a watertight door—a ghost nicknamed Half-Hatch Harry.

From the Queen's Salon—a former dining area—came reports of the ghost of a young woman, dancing alone, to music no one else could hear.

The "Screaming Sailor" terrified those who ventured too near the bow at night. Many believe that is where the tormented spirit of a young sailor killed during the crash at sea during World War II lingers.

Throughout her service, the *Queen Mary* made 1,001 trans-Atlantic crossings.

And of course, there is Jackie. By far the most famous of the *Queen Mary*'s ghosts, this spirit has been reported in many areas of the ship. She is most frequently seen in the pool area, where some believe she may have drowned.

Most who see Jackie describe her as playful and full of mischief. Her games of "hide-and-seek" are legendary. But her pleas for her long-lost mother leave many feeling heartbroken afterward.

Is the *Queen Mary* really haunted? Does Jackie really roam her decks, searching for her mother? Or does the dark history of the grand ship simply inspire the imaginations of those who visit? We may never know for sure.

TIMELINE

December 1, 1930—The first keel piece of the *Queen Mary* is assembled.

September 26, 1934—The RMS *Queen Mary* is launched, and receives her official name.

May 27, 1936—Leaving Southampton, the *Queen Mary* makes her maiden voyage for Cherbourg, France, and then New York.

1939—The *Queen Mary* makes her final voyage before entering war service.

September 3, 1939—Great Britain and France declare war on Germany.

March 1, 1940—The *Queen Mary* is called into service.

March 21, 1940—The ship leaves for Australia to be outfitted for war time.

October 2, 1942—The *Queen Mary* and HMS *Curacoa* collide, cutting the smaller *Curacoa* in half. Hundreds of the *Curacoa's* sailors lose their lives.

May 8, 1945—The Allies accept Germany's surrender, ending World War II.

September 24, 1946—The *Queen Mary* begins her final military voyage, leaving from Halifax and arriving in Southampton three days later.

July 31, 1947—The ship leaves Southampton for New York on her first voyage after the war.

July 10, 1966—According to legend, John Peddler is killed during a watertight drill.

October 31, 1967—Leaving from Southampton, England, the ship makes her final voyage to Long Beach, California.

December 9, 1967—The ship is retired and dry docked in Long Beach.

November 2, 1972—The first hotel rooms open aboard the ship.

January 12, 2004—The *Queen Mary 2*, named for the *Queen Mary,* makes her maiden voyage.

February 23, 2006—The *Queen Mary 2* arrives at Long Beach. The *Queen Mary* and the *Queen Mary 2* whistle at each other in salute. This is the first and only time the two ships make contact.

GLOSSARY

Art Deco (ART DEK-oh)—style of art or architecture that was popular in the 1930s

boiler (BOY-luhr)—a tank that boils water to produce steam

claustrophobic (KLOSS-truh-FO-bik)—the fear of being in closed or narrow spaces

concussion (kuhn-KUH-shuhn)—an injury to the brain caused by a hard blow to the head

disorient (dis-OH-ree-EHNT)—to lose the sense of time, place, or identity

gangway (GANG-way)—plank used for getting on and off a boat or ship

hallucination (huh-loo-suh-NAY-shuhn)—something seen that is not really there

hatch (HACH)—a covered hole in a floor, deck, door, wall, or ceiling

hull (HUL)—the main body of a boat

hypnotic (hip-NOH-tik)—a method that puts someone in a trancelike state

keel (KEEL)—the wooden or metal piece that runs along the bottom of a boat

mystical (miss-TIK-uhl)—something that is spiritual or supernatural in nature

ominous (OM-uh-nuhss)—describes something that gives the impression that something bad is going to happen

ornate (OR-nay-t)—elaborately or excessively decorated

paranormal (pair-uh-NOR-muhl)—having to do with an unexplained event that has no scientific explanation

promenade (PROM-uh-NAH-d)—a place to take a leisurely walk or stroll

prow (PROW)—the front part of a boat or ship

purser (PUR-suhr)—a ship's officer in charge of documents and passengers' valuables

renovate (REH-no-vate)—to restore something to good condition

salon (SUH-lahn)—an elegant hall to exhibit art, and for fashionable people to gather

stateroom (STAYT-room)—a first-class passenger's sleeping quarters on a ship

OTHER PATHS TO EXPLORE

In this book you've seen how terrifying being alone in a haunted place can be. But haunted places can mean different things to different people. Seeing an experience from many points of view is an important part of understanding it.

Here are a few ideas for other haunted points of view to explore:

- Ghost hunters have studied the *Queen Mary* intensely. With their electronic gear, they've discovered hints that there just might be something supernatural. Imagine you're a ghost hunter aboard the ship. Where would you explore first? Would the experience be terrifying? Exciting? Or both?

- What if you were a tour guide aboard the *Queen Mary* and one of your tourists became lost on the ship? Would you go after them, or wait to see if they turned up?

- Many people helped build the *Queen Mary*. What might working on such a huge ship have been like? Would you be afraid to visit the ship, or would it feel like a fun reminder of your past?

READ MORE

Chandler, Matt. *Bachelor's Grove Cemetery and Other Haunted Places of the Midwest.* North Mankato, Minn.: Capstone Press, 2014.

Henneberg, Susan. *Investigating Ghosts and the Spirit World.* New York: Britannica Educational Publishing in Association with Rosen Educational Services, 2015.

Shea, Therese. *Haunted!: The Queen Mary.* New York: Gareth Stevens Publishing, 2013.

INTERNET SITES

Use FactHound to find Internet sites related to this book. All of the sites on FactHound have been researched by our staff.

Here's all you do:
Visit *www.facthound.com*
Type in this code: 9781515725787

INDEX